The Curse of Urvashi

The Curse of Urvashi

(Inspired by the *Virata Parva* of the *Mahabharata*,
Bhasa's *Mahabharata*-based plays and
Anupam Kumar's *Brihanalla*)

V Balakrishnan

ZERO DEGREE PUBLISHING

Title: The Curse of Urvashi
Author's name: V Balakrishnan

Published By: Zero Degree Publishing

Zero Degree Publishing
No. 55(7), R Block, 6th Avenue,
Anna Nagar West,
Chennai - 600040
Ph: 9840065000

e mail: zerodegreepublishing@gmail.com
website: www. zerodegreepublishing.com
Printed at Manipal Technologies, India.

First Edition by Zero Degree Publishing: December 2021
ISBN: 978-81-954399-1-1
ZDP Title: 41

Cover Design: Meera Sitaraman
Cover Photo: C Vishwajith
Typeset: Vidhya Velayudham
Printed at Manipal Technologies, India

Playwright's Note

In my first year at the National School of Drama, we were part of a play titled *Brihanalla* by a brilliant young playwright, Anupam Kumar. What fascinated me most about the play was the conflict created between Uttara and Arjuna. This served as a prominent inspiration in the writing of a few scenes in this play.

The events described in this play do not necessarily occur in the great epic; some have been inspired from folk versions through the centuries.

This version of the play premiered at the Alliance Française of Madras in 2018 with the following cast and crew:

BRIHANALLA (ARJUNA): Meera Sitaraman/Shakthi Ramani
KRISHNA: V Balakrishnan
URVASHI: Nithya Ramachandran
DRAUPADI: Roshini Sridhar
UTTARA, BHOOMINJAY UTTARA KUMAR: Aparna Kumar
DANCERS: Shivangi Singh, Niveditha
MUSIC: Vishwa Bharath, Srivaralaxmi Maya
LIGHTING DESIGN: Janani Venkateswaran
DESIGN AND DIRECTION: V Balakrishnan

The representations in movement were inspired by traditional folk dance forms – Khukuri dance, Devarattam and Therukoothu, in the initial performances.

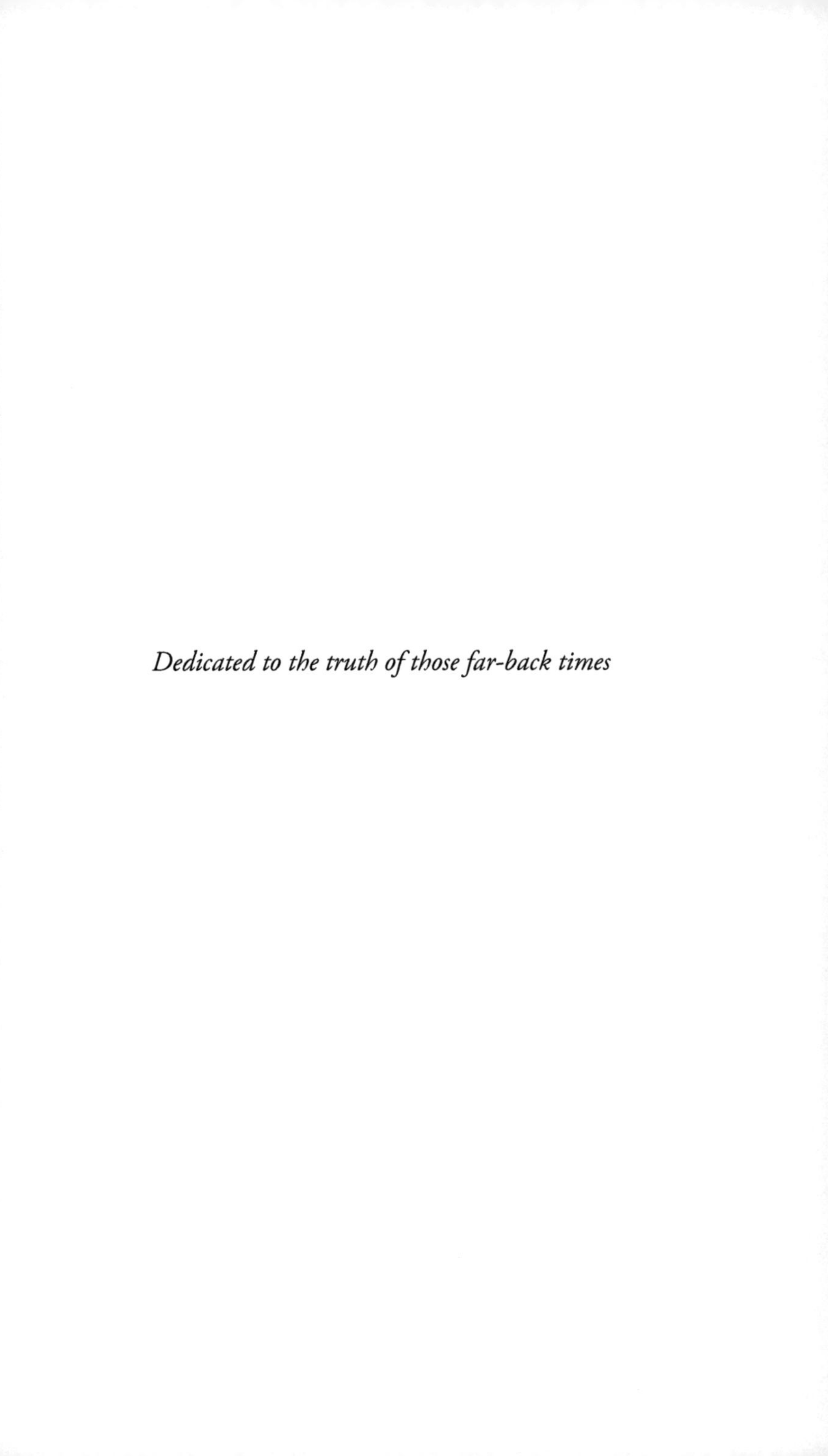

Dedicated to the truth of those far-back times

The Future

Scene One

ARJUNA:

Krishna is going to die.
He called me to explain why,
while his kinsmen slaughter themselves
with lusty blows of the reeds growing by the river side,
drunk in the stupor of wine and ego,
Krishna has chosen to die like an animal.
An animal about to be hunted
by a crouching forester
with a brand-new arrow.
The rest of his clan
crushed each other's skulls with iron pestles,
strangled the eyes out of the sockets.
Not the first war where brother killed brother.
I saw Satyaki, my best student, die.

Kritavarma, who led the Narayani, died.
Pradyumna, Samba, Gada, everyone died.
Krishna has chosen to retire
to a secluded clearing in the forest,
where he awaits the arrow that was forged from the metal
that could not be ground to fine powder,
to mingle in the ocean waters,
after having been delivered
from the charade and body of his arrogant son,
who lay screaming as the mace slid out of his orifice,
widened by the curse of the wandering Rishis.
Krishna called me from Hastinapura
to take to safety his many wives.
The senior ones refused to accompany me.
The fragrance of his funeral pyre seduces them for sure.
As I made my way through the forest,
bandits attacked us, common bandits attacked us;
they stole the women from me.
I was not even able to string my bow.
I remember
Krishna wanted me to return the Gandiva to Varuna
after the carnage at Kurukshetra.
I desisted.
Today, I was not able to gather the string at the nock,
not able to notch one arrow.
The mantras slipped away from my memory
like butter from a child's palm.
Mantras of terrible destruction,
taught by Pashupati, Drona, Indra,
all eluded my memory.

The syllables refused to conjoin to create the force.
The words did not add up.
The metre fell apart.
Karna, I finally know how you felt.
The bandits spared me,
but took the women gleefully.
Many walked away with them of their own accord.
Krishna's wives have been taken away
by bandits and robbers.
Women he had saved from the king of the North,
the women who married him in ecstasy
have been all lost by me.
Here I am, hidden in the bushes,
unable to face him,
or seek his words of comfort.
Krishna has settled under that huge tree
and I can see the arrow that the hunter aims at his feet,
mistaking it for the face of a deer.
I am paralysed, time holds me frozen
like the chariot wheel that sunk in the mire,
where I was the arrow
and another was to die.
Now, Krishna sighs and smiles,
and my mouth cannot form words to scream.
Where did we go wrong?
Time has slipped away from our grasp completely.
Krishna is going to die,
but it is my life that passes before my eyes.
I have lived a life of punishment,
one incident leading to another.

None of my prowess was of avail.
All those years of practice held no sway.
Everyone I faced was better than me,
and had to be put away by trickery.
No new story I am telling here.
You know them all by name and lore,
some forgotten in the thirty six years
that have passed since the war.
Bhishma, Drona, Karna,
Jayadratha, Bhoorishravas…
I broke the rules of men.
I broke the rules of nature.
Krishna was cursed to die,
and so was I.
Long, long ago when
I went to the immortal world in my mortal frame,
and paid for it with pain,
I broke the rules of the gods.
Urvashi cursed me in the worst possible way,
and despite Indra's intervention,
the curse lingered over my life; still does.
Then I remember there was another
who was angry with me.
I am old before my time,
feeble, a travesty of what I was,
relegated to tales and folklore
of the man who defeated Karna.
Urvashi cursed me to live without virility.
The curse spread all over my body.
The curse stayed and multiplied.

I sensed fear, I was defeated.
Today, I am seeing my worst fear realised.
Krishna is going to die,
and I can't save him.
Maybe, that's the way he planned it,
to remind me of his words.
Words spoken over eighteen days
now rendered to one practical test.
Nature is still.
Even silence is silenced.
Krishna smiles, and heaves,
and in that heave, he has gathered his life breath,
ready to exit his body.
The hunter's mouth is drooling.
He sees a deer where Krishna's feet rest,
and he draws his bowstring with ease
to his ear.
That arrow has as its killing head
the piece that could not be rendered to dust.
He releases his arrow.
Krishna will now die.

The Past

Scene Two

Urvashi:

Arjuna, you stand here in the dark,
amidst the dying cacophony
of a war you won with ease.
Now, you must put out the flames of another war
that rages with you for its cause.
While the performance was underway,
your eyes were dreaming beyond the stage,
beyond the etiquette of the actor and the spectator,
close to bursting with joy,
and your eyes were on me, my limbs, my breasts, and face.
You desired me with a raging flame,
and I felt I wanted you too.
I love you, and I love you with joy that is unbridled
and threatens to flow
beyond the modest garb of silken vestry.

This night is darker,
for I have drawn the veil of love around it,
and we are protected
from the ears and eyes of Indra's spies.
Upon this ground that you tread with your weight,
let us with love and burning lust, this thirst satiate.

ARJUNA:

Rather that you curse me to the hell
reserved for those with incestuous dreams
than appropriate my steadfast gaze
to be one of lust and sexual whims.
I am Partha, son of Pandu, who was the son of
Vichitraveerya, who was the son of Shantanu,
and as I trace the steps of my lineage, with aplomb I stop at
Vikrama, also known as Pururava,
whom you knew
and called the best among them all, Purushottama.
I have descended from him,
who was your lover, who was your other.
Urvashi, you are the most revered in my heart, my mother.
I looked upon your form not to covet it like a beast in heat,
but to admire the progenitor of us warriors complete.

URVASHI:

Don't you see what has happened to me?
I have come to you with lust and in season.
You are a man, and you need to make love to me,
satiate me and allow my fires to cool.
To make love with consent is sweeter than honey,
and I feel this is not lust kindled anew

but a passion I have been hoarding since I knew you.
Let me make it simple, for you seem to fear laws and rules.
I am not asking you to be my consort or husband,
I need you now, and I am within the rights
afforded by nature.
I have approached you by the laws of the maker,
and you need to play your part,
as the other half of nature's delight.

Arjuna:

Any man would leap at this offer of yours;
to be sought by the best among women,
even the gods vie for that.
But I am a mortal, a man
who follows the strictures of becoming and unbecoming;
and to seek one's mother in bodily want is despicable,
and will not go unpunished by the makers of law.
Love is but a whim that they with leisure indulge in.
To pleasure the body is but the avocation
of those with knowledge unattained.
The makers of heaven and earth have a thousand eyes,
and they are watching us like eagles.
No Urvashi, mother, there is no hope
and you should harbour none.
I will not be to you what my ancestor was.
Please go away.

Urvashi:

Of all the men I have known,
you are the strangest.
I am a woman who approaches you

in need and want and desire.
You cannot by law refuse me, and lay waste to my season.
What stops you that you hide behind inane reasons?
What prompts you to seek refuge in moral mire?
You hide more truths than common mortals require.

ARJUNA:

Pray, Urvashi, pray!
Yes, I did not reveal to you
the greater contravention you committed
in having approached me in heat,
for even the gods don't forgive that transgression,
and by not mentioning it,
I chose to save you from damnation.
In time that does not exist to the casual eye,
that is a continuum of irresistible eternity,
with my brother Narayana, I, Nara, was meditating.
And to answer Indra and his cheap thrills,
we created a girl child from our thighs.
That girl was you, whom Indra requested for himself.
Coming from the thigh of Narayana,
you became Urvashi,
and are like my own creation.

URVASHI:

Quite common for men to make women,
daughters and mothers,
when their masculinity fears to embrace
the truth of their redundant virility
that cannot serve the purpose of fecundity.
As usual, be silent.

And the gods too, observe, are silent.
Arjuna, I curse you.
I curse you, not out of anger,
but because I need an heir for this desire
that has burst open from my pores,
and will drown all that is pure.
I curse you, Arjuna!
May this masculinity which you hide behind
and use as an excuse for your rights and wrongs,
this lineage yarn you spin to make me feel like a whore,
this father figure you suddenly become
to make me feel low,
well, may this masculinity then diminish
and may your loins lose their fire.
Live life now, son of all those great names you took,
as a being of no sexual feeling.
Bear the body of a man, and its attributes,
but no sensation will trouble you anymore.
And then maybe you can preach morals with gain,
where a desperate woman need never bargain,
over laws that even the lower creatures
are aware of and respect.
You have broken those rules of nature.
You have made a woman
who came to you in sexual longing,
feel despicable, and like a child
which soils itself for knowing no better.
You have made me feel ashamed and humiliated.
So let my words hold.
Be you Nara or Narayana himself,

be you Indra's son or Puru's lineage,
spend the rest of your life without
the joy of sexual longings, feelings or manly wants.
Be the dry vacuum of nothingness.
You quote destiny
where I sought necessity.
You mistook invincibility to be fate, necessity a quagmire,
but now suffer, as a being of no sexual desire.

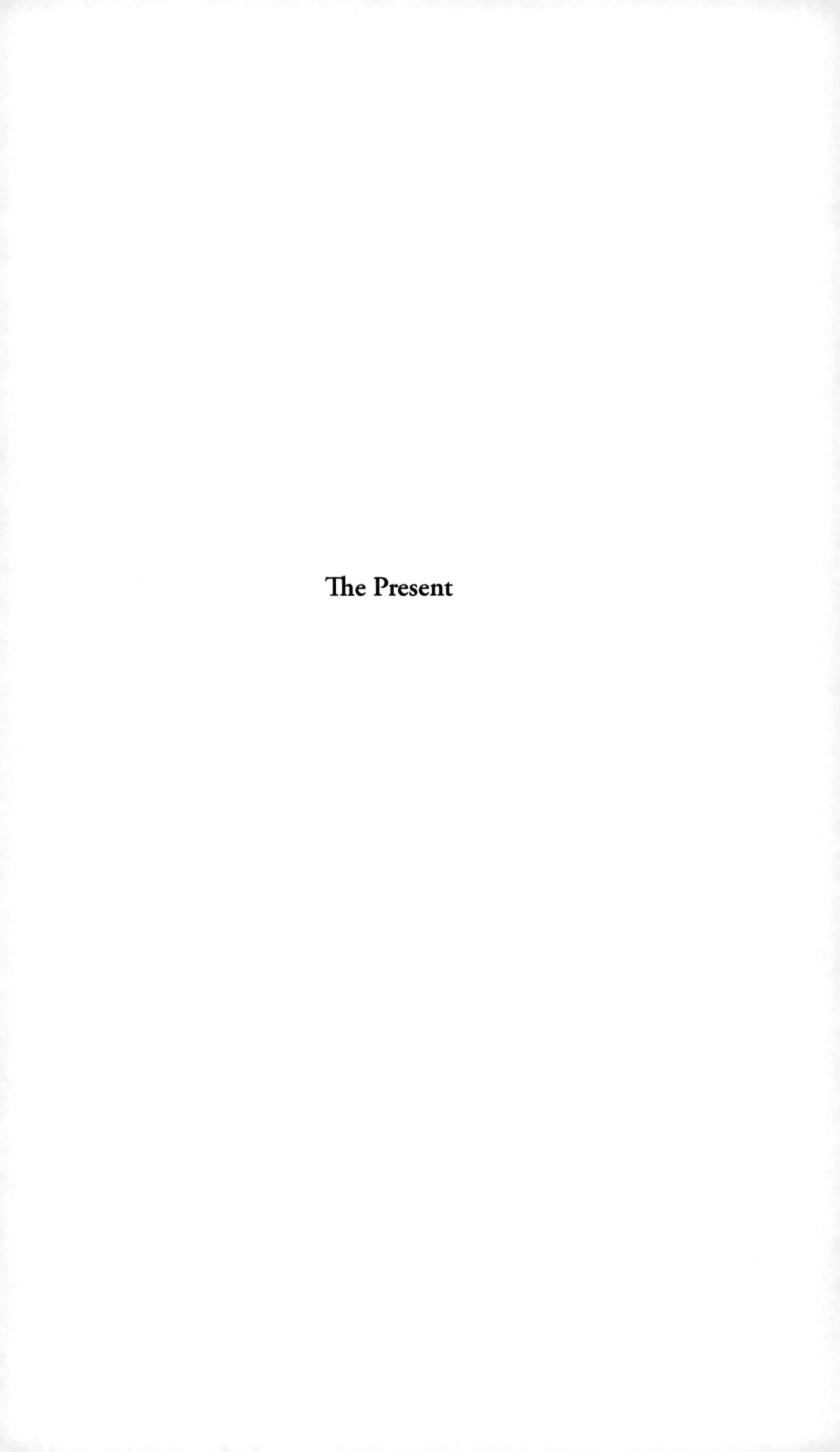

The Present

Scene Three

DRAUPADI:

If luck is a factor that runs our lives and fate,
then I am the unluckiest to have walked the earth.
Did I murder children or kill my teachers,
that life commits me to such a terrible punishment?
I am a mockery of fate.
Reduced from the ruler of the earth to a maid.
I pestle my anger as I grind the perfumes
the king insists on for his depraved body.
I lived without knowing fear.
Now, I shake for I am afraid.
Kichaka makes me tremble
with his lascivious summons.
His sister offers me to him like a festival gift.
I would rather die than live to be treated like trash.

Krishna:

(*dressed in feminine attire*)
In living we nurture hope.
The pond dries to fill again.
They who await, prevail,
and better times are bestowed.

Draupadi:

What happened, Krishna?
Has Arjuna been your inspiration,
or did you too offend some woman?

Krishna:

I admire your élan
in dispensing with formality and etiquette.
Don't you want to know
what I am doing here,
or why this elegant guise?

Draupadi:

I am tired of living.

Krishna:

Why? What tires you?
Pounding flowers for perfume?
I could think of worse afflictions.

Draupadi:

I was born of fire.
I am the princess of Panchala,
the queen of Indraprastha,
and I am quaking with fear.

A bully wants me for his bed,
and his sister offers me as easily
as a sweet her brother demanded.
Five demigods married me,
and not one can stand by me.

KRISHNA:

Fate is most demanding
when better times are close, Draupadi.
Your husbands have a mission
bigger than you and I.
This earth has carried venom for ages now,
and your husbands must cleanse it for her life to be renewed.
What is the worth of your life and mine,
when the whole earth clamours for emancipation?

DRAUPADI:

Give me the assurance that noble day will arrive,
and I will pass each minute without complaining
of all its abuses and agonies.
I do not protest that I suffer.
But is this the future of the earth?
Give me your word,
and I will nurture hope.
I will die and be reborn each day,
but I will await a better world.
And yes, despite my earlier protestations,
my curiosity is awakened.
What brings you here, away from the capital?
Is it not dangerous?

KRISHNA:

Duryodhana still seeks the Pandavas in worthy spaces,
like a man searching for a lost ring in a pond.
His net is well spread,
but he is nowhere close to the truth of your hiding place.
And to answer your inquisition,
listen carefully.
There is a murmur in the air.
The forces of humans and nature are gathering strength
to march for righteousness.
All those who oppose it will die.
Your patrons of today will become your suppliants.
Those who wound you today
will, without mercy, perish,
overthrown casually like sifting sand.

DRAUPADI:

But when will that day arrive?
What is it about my life that draws
ill luck to it like a charm?
My husbands are fulfilling some childhood fantasy,
escaping into the realms of dreams,
role-playing as menial servants
and teachers of dance and music.
Where is their prosperity, their splendour, their glory?
They have tragically forgotten their duties.

KRISHNA:

They don't sleep, Draupadi.
They are not unaware.
They have been impaired

by their decisions, and the rules
that they have set for themselves.
They can destroy all they see in front of them,
but that won't serve what nature wants.
They seem fallen and asleep,
but the serpent feigns
when it coils.
When the time arrives,
they will unleash themselves
with such ferocity that
you will be avenged and more,
and the earth breathe in joy.

DRAUPADI:

If they are what you make them out to be,
then are they casually turning a blind eye
to the state of their wife?
If nothing else, where is their manly pride?
When their wife is being desired by another man,
they coil to recoil?

KRISHNA:

Draupadi, I came here
to tell you to be prepared.
There is a game being set
for the final onslaught.
Do not harness yourself to despair
at this pertinent moment.
Hold and wait like an arrow at its fullest draw,
for the mark is set, and the string is taut.
You will not be disappointed.

Draupadi:

I have been shamed, humiliated,
and dishonoured by Kichaka.
Why should I not reach out
to Drupada and Dhrishtadyumna?
They will destroy this kingdom
and kill the charioteer.
What is this tiny kingdom to the Panchalas?
Did Urvashi curse Arjuna alone, or all five?
Where is their wrath, their prowess and energy?
Dishonourable they are. Cowards.
How do I blame Kichaka for acting without morality,
for having forgotten his duty,
when my husbands and the king they serve
of the same manifold are guilty?
I was kicked and spat upon, Krishna, in public.
In fear for my husbands' guises,
I could not take your name this time.
Or I would make the Matsyas piss with fear,
like Dhritarashtra and his cronies.
Why am I doing all this? For what?
I do not desire to live.
My husbands cannot protect me,
nor have any power to do so.
Arjuna is happy and gratified,
surrounded by women all the while,
wearing bracelets and bangles,
singing songs and correcting acting nuances.
I do not wish to live.

Krishna:

Bhima will have to kill Kichaka.
Let me tell you a story not well known.
Duryodhana, Kichaka, Shalya, and Bhima,
with Balarama make up the famous five mace wielders.
Shalya, of course, being a senior student of Balarama.
The other three were always jealous of each other's prowess.
Balarama drew a ring of protection around them,
for there was a curse
that one would kill all.
Bhima has promised to kill Duryodhana.
So he will have to kill Kichaka as well.
Tonight, approach Bhima and instigate him.
With amour, seduce him.
He loves you the most.
He will break his word to his brother,
and he will break Kichaka's neck.

Draupadi:

Will you be visiting Arjuna,
for he is the one—along with Yudhishthira—
who pressed me to keep silent and suffer?
They fear the discovery of their clandestine operation,
and the prospect of another exile.
They would rather that Kichaka live,
and they be undiscovered,
so Duryodhana may die,
than see me safe.
Bhima may go against Yudhishthira's order of silence,
but he won't cross Arjuna's erudition,

in making the strategies of war.
Bhima will weep with me,
but action will demand Arjuna's assent.
Will you be meeting him, your friend?

KRISHNA:

I will. I need to see him.
I need to prepare him for another war.
You must tell Kichaka you will meet him tonight.
I will ask Arjuna to decorate the dancing hall,
for that will be the altar of the sacrifice,
the beginning of the extravagant flow of warrior blood.
Draupadi, prepare for war.
Kichaka will be the first offering,
killed by Bhima tonight.
He will set the stage for the performance
of many an act and scene,
to follow in poetic flow.
Arrange to meet Kichaka tonight
in the hall where Arjuna teaches music and dance.
And there, Bhima will meet him in your guise.
Tonight, not one but three men will roam
in the garb of women,
for the confluence of prakriti and purusha is needed
to create and destroy.
And this trinity will suffice
to rid the earth of its excruciating pain.
Accept your new circumstances as bold and happy ones,
for now it is redemption time for the whole earth.
Tonight, Kichaka will die.

Scene Four

Brihanalla:

Is that you Krishna?

Krishna:

Is that you Arjuna?

Brihanalla:

Why are you dressed in the colours of mourning? Has someone died?

Krishna:

No, but someone is going to this night… here, in this dancing hall.

Brihanalla:

Your words strike an ominous note.
You shroud in mystery,
something that should be revealed instantly.

KRISHNA:

Have my spies been keeping you informed
of what is brewing in the court of Hastinapura?

BRIHANALLA:

Regularly. And that is why your presence is disturbing my thoughts.

KRISHNA:

Kichaka has broken the rules of etiquette.
He has behaved unworthily of a host.

BRIHANALLA:

I know, and I swallow the bile
that threatens to burn him and his siblings.
I fear for my elder brother
and the rules we agreed to abide by.
Kichaka will die, but in due time
and in the pertinent place.

KRISHNA:

Tonight, he will die, killed by Bhima.
Once Draupadi approaches Bhima,
Bhima will seek your counsel.
You will advise him to do it,
and here in this hall of dance.

BRIHANALLA:

Krishna, are you insane?
We cannot afford to be discovered.
Not now, when only a month remains
for the exile to be exhausted.

We have suffered indignity and insults for thirteen years,
and now a month remains between us and our birthright.
Why this counsel now, to expose ourselves?

KRISHNA:

Duryodhana has the support of all the kings on earth.
His reign is a good one.
The people are happy and content.
They live glorious days.
People have forgotten you.
The rules of the dice game are now abstruse.
When you return with the conditions fulfilled,
Duryodhana will reject it as invalid,
or create a million loopholes to deny what is yours.
That is certain.
War is certain.
But war needs machinery, soldiers, and money.
You need allies.
Allies will assemble when they know
you are marked to win and rule.
We need a dress rehearsal.
A battle for all to know why the Pandavas must be feared.
A battle for your strength to be exposed,
so allies and friends will renew agreements and accords,
and stand by your banner.
When the battle commences,
every serf to his manor.

BRIHANALLA:

And killing Kichaka will do that?

KRISHNA:

The slaying of Kichaka will be the inspiration
that will hustle the Kurus to the plains,
that will be the call for the hyenas,
and will gather the princes to be slain.
Virata's cows have always been the envy of Hastinapura.
You will ascend to protect the king,
and the world will know
that the Pandavas have defeated the Kurus,
and must be given their rightful dues.

BRIHANALLA:

But the time that remains…
Why let them cheat us once again
on a technical point?

KRISHNA:

Fifteen days for the news to reach Kurujangala;
fifteen for them to march to the Matsya plains.
Add a few for the council of war and other diplomacies.
You will be safe from all points of technicality.
The period of disguise will be over and done.

BRIHANALLA:

Krishna, we need time to rustle our spirits,
and practice our skills too.

KRISHNA:

I give you a month.
But then it's only you.
The rest have been in practice and getting better too.

I hope you have not forgotten the skills of war,
or counterfeited them with the craft of the stage.
Gestures and expressions are great,
but can't be the vehicle of stoic rage.

Brihanalla:

Lead me through your plan again?

Krishna:

Tonight, let there be no late rehearsals.
Keep the little girls away.
Let no instrument which could assist Kichaka be nearby,
and tomorrow raise the alarm late,
so Bhima has time to recuperate.
Give yourself a good alibi, and stay in the temple of Kali.
Offer her worship that is due this season.
And then, what will be, will be.

Brihanalla:

Krishna, the curse of Urvashi
has liberated me in many ways.
Teaching dance and music has allowed me
to rest my troubled mind and ruminate.
We don't need the kingdom and its gold.
We need freedom, and we need space.
If the massacre of the earth can be avoided
by us, the Pandavas, remaining in exile,
then would it be wrong to desire so?

Krishna:

It would require me many days
to afford a clinical answer,

to indulge in proper deliberation.
Some other time maybe,
when we can afford eighteen days?

Brihanalla:

Stay safe and sharp, Krishna.
Kichaka is easily mesmerised,
and you sport a worthy feminine disguise.

Krishna:

You think I am in disguise?

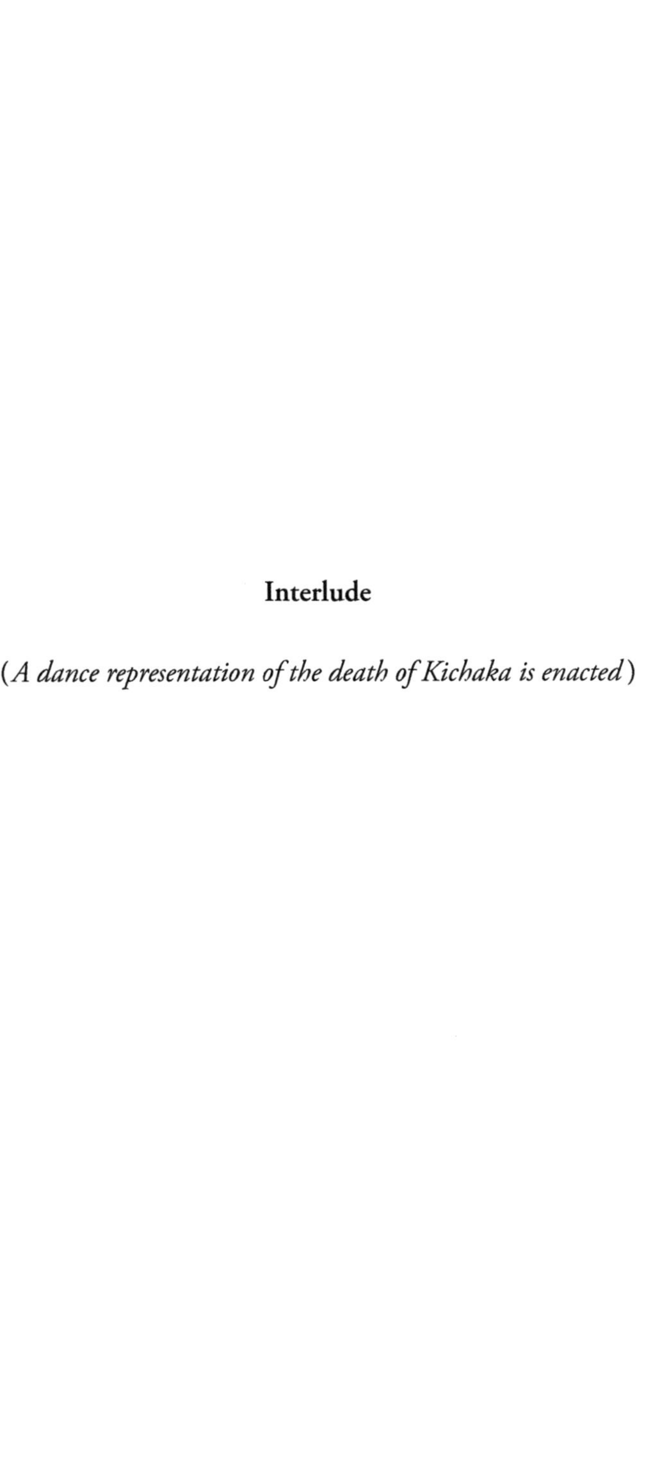

Interlude

(*A dance representation of the death of Kichaka is enacted*)

Scene Five

BRIHANALLA:

Princess Uttara, did you wish to see me?

UTTARA:

Yes, I am not comfortable studying in the dance hall…
My uncle was murdered there.
I wanted to tell you
that we can continue the lessons here in my room,
if it's all the same to you.

BRIHANALLA:

The palace will be in mourning for a week at least.
We will commence
after the period of silence is observed.
For now, I will serve you
with whatever you desire.

The king has ordered me to stay near you
as your protector.

UTTARA:

Do you fear the death of the general
places us in peril too?
I heard he was killed by beings of another region,
whose wife he had insulted.
I do not mourn his punishment, that was just.
But he was my uncle,
and as my uncle, I remember him and mourn him.

BRIHANALLA:

You have my condolences.

UTTARA:

Are you sure?
You don't seem too perturbed.

BRIHANALLA:

I mourn him in the capacity I knew him.

UTTARA:

Hmm…
Yesterday there was so much I wished to ask you,
and talk about with you.
Then this news of death.
But the gloom has settled, and I am calm.
Would you like to instruct me now?

BRIHANALLA:

That is my duty.
I am your teacher and your protector too.

Please ask me what you wish.
What is troubling you,
Math, Science or Logic?

UTTARA:

Maybe a mix of all and more…
Please hand me that bowl.
It contains some sandal paste,
and I have a bad headache.

BRIHANALLA:

May I apply some
on your forehead?

UTTARA:

Apply some on my shoulders and back too.
I feel stiff and fatigued.

BRIHANALLA:

You are tense.

UTTARA:

Brihanalla, please loosen the drapes,
and apply it well.

BRIHANALLA:

Princess… would you like me to call your personal retinue?

UTTARA:

This is the day of mourning…
If my mother knows I am getting a sandal paste massage,
she will be aghast.
No, you do it, unless you don't wish to.

Brihanalla:

I am at your service, Princess.
It is my job.

Uttara:

Your hands are so graceful.
The way they feel upon my skin…
It is a strange relation we have, Brihanalla.
You are my teacher, my mentor,
and my servant too.

Brihanalla:

That was the service I was offered,
when I asked your father for work.

Uttara:

You are my elder… maybe it's not right
for me to ask you to do this…
I am sorry, you may stop and leave.

Brihanalla:

It is well within the services
I am to provide,
if you so desire.

Uttara:

So, teacher, will you enlighten me?

Brihanalla:

What would you like enlightenment on?

Uttara:

Humans, relations, feelings, and emotions.

BRIHANALLA:

Not my forté,
but I will do my best.

UTTARA:

You are neither man nor woman?

BRIHANALLA:

That's limited in perception.
We all have qualities that we call masculine…
and those we call feminine,
and those that, in our limitations, we have not defined.

UTTARA:

The third nature?

BRIHANALLA:

Who placed masculinity and femininity as first and second?
No, Princess, this is more political than biological.

UTTARA:

But what would be your choice of gender?
If you could choose to be assigned with one,
would you rather be a complete man or a complete woman?

BRIHANALLA:

Neither.

UTTARA:

Explain. What does that mean?

BRIHANALLA:

Completeness is not ordained by nature.

If anything, to be incomplete is nature's way,
so we may evolve the way
we get stimulated to define ourselves.
To have the body of a man or the body of a woman
is limited to procreation.
Beyond that there is no bifurcation.

UTTARA:

And love? Have you fallen in love?
Was it with a man or a woman or both?

BRIHANALLA:

Love is to participate in one's growth.

UTTARA:

And sex?

BRIHANALLA:

To procreate.

UTTARA:

Liar… sex with consent is like honey…
I heard someone say that to me in a dream.
Does a person look attractive because I love them?
Or do I love them because I am attracted to them?

BRIHANALLA:

I have no idea.

UTTARA:

Have you never fallen in love?

BRIHANALLA:

I have.

UTTARA:

Do you love me?

BRIHANALLA:

Of course, I do.

UTTARA:

You love me but do not desire me.

BRIHANALLA:

These questions are not within the purview of our relations.
Princess Uttara, your father will not be pleased.

UTTARA:

Last question… is it possible
to love someone without sexual attraction?

BRIHANALLA:

I just answered that question.

UTTARA:

Not for you, for me.

BRIHANALLA:

Are you in love?

UTTARA:

Answer me.

BRIHANALLA:

Yes, Princess, it is possible for you
to love someone, without physically desiring them.

UTTARA:

Not "Princess", but Uttara.
Uttara who has fallen in love
with her teacher, Brihanalla.

BRIHANALLA:

I love you too, Princess Uttara.

UTTARA:

No Brihanalla… you don't…

BRIHANALLA:

What do you mean?

UTTARA:

I want you to embrace me.

BRIHANALLA:

No, Princess… It is punishable by death.

UTTARA:

I would gladly die after embracing you once.

BRIHANALLA:

Punishable by death for me… not you.

UTTARA:

You know it's against the law to refuse a woman
who comes to you on her own accord?

BRIHANALLA:

That rule is for men.
I am not one.

UTTARA:

Did you know the prince of Panchala, Shikhandi,
was born a woman, and later became a man?
He married too,
and has a daughter.
Maybe you too can hope,
and gain the way he did.
Become a man or a woman…

BRIHANALLA:

I am happy the way I am,
for the ways of the gods are unknown.
If I am ordained to be who I am,
then I trust the greater plan of destiny.
To rupture the fabric of nature's weave
can be dangerous,
and to shift the proceedings of fate
lead to unbecoming turbulence.

UTTARA:

Even if it will make me happy, you won't do it?

BRIHANALLA:

Will you want me to do it if it will make me unhappy?

UTTARA:

Am I ugly or not attractive enough for you?
I am the princess of Matsya.
We are derived from the gods themselves.
Like Draupadi and Dhrishtadyumna, *ayonijas*[1].

---

1 One who was not born from the womb

My grandfather was the favourite of the gods.
We are related to the Kurus and the Panchalas,
and yet you reject me.

Brihanalla:

Princess Uttara, I am not worthy
of someone as precious as you.
And if you are not interested in your lessons,
then may I leave?

Uttara:

I love you, Brihanalla,
and maybe I am wrong in asking you
to change for me.
But I love you.
Please don't despise me.

Brihanalla:

Of course I don't despise you, Princess.
I told you I love you.

Uttara:

Hypothetically, if some day,
by god's grace you become a man,
then will you make love to me?
Maybe marry me?

Brihanalla:

Hypotheses are not in our curriculum,
and you are dreaming, Princess.
Maybe the season of spring is intoxicating you,
and poor you has only me

to see and be with.
Maybe I will suggest to the king that it's time your
paintings made the rounds of the houses of kings.

UTTARA:

No, I won't succumb to something inane.
I want a competition.
Like the ones Krishna and Arjuna participated in
where Karna can venture in too.
I want the heart to strain its sweet longings for me,
and draw the bow of destiny.
An endeavour which must drain the contestant,
and still he must reign.

BRIHANALLA:

And who among those three old men
would you like to win the day?

UTTARA:

None of them.
I would dream you would string a bow
and shoot a fish,
and make me yours.

BRIHANALLA:

We are not allowed to wield weapons.
And, Princess, like I mentioned before,
you are dreaming.

UTTARA:

Brihanalla, I harbour no dreams…
only hopes that you become a man and marry me.

If that's not possible,
then you will stay with me till the end of days.

BRIHANALLA:

I bless you, Princess,
and yes, if the gods wish,
you will stay with me till the end of days.

Scene Six

KRISHNA:

Arjuna, we need to re-plan.
There has been an unprecedented move by the Kauravas.
The death of Kichaka had its desired effect.
Bhima's hand is suspected.
Duryodhana senses Virata's helplessness,
and he salivates to acquire his cows.
He commanded Drona to assemble the army
when Susharma of the Trigartas
added to his plan.
The new strategy is to attack from two fronts.
The first onslaught will be from the south…
That will be manned by Susharma and his brothers.
This will be a fierce one,
which Virata and his army will rush to hold,

leaving the northern plains unguarded.
And then to add to his coffers,
as punishment for hiding you five brothers,
Duryodhana will make away with the bovine.
Now, he does not expect the Pandavas
to reveal themselves in the war with Susharma.
But the second attack he knows
will leave you with no choice
but to come to the front and fight.

BRIHANALLA:

If he fears the northern attack as the more pertinent one,
then his army will be of stature too.
Who will he bring to the battle with him…?
Too many or too few?

KRISHNA:

The usual suspects.
Bhishma, Drona, Karna, Ashwatthama and Dushasana.
Each with their personal contingent.
But the surprise factor will be Abhimanyu and Lakshmana.
He is making the Kuru cubs cut their teeth early.

BRIHANALLA:

You let Abhimanyu go?

KRISHNA:

What choice does the maternal uncle have
when the paters demand their rights?
Abhimanyu belongs to the house of the Kurus
and he fights from their side.

BRIHANALLA:

The cattle are obviously his contingency plan.
To tell the world why he tread on Virata's toes,
if we fail to reveal ourselves.
But the exile is almost over
and the next moon will complete the terms and conditions.
Duryodhana marches well,
but he marches to a futile endeavour.
Krishna, your predictions hold right.
Virata will be alienated,
and will sway to our side.

KRISHNA:

Arjuna, there is a clause.
The battle of Virata must not
to the Kauravas spell total loss.
Duryodhana must face more indignity than defeat.
Wound his pride… his ego.
But he should return in one piece.
The war of the Kuru clan should not bear fruition
on the plains of Matsya's frontiers.
Save that for the area of the five lakes.
The count is too low now.
I need the armies of the world to gather.
I need the war to be on a larger front.
The world must notice that the Pandavas
are not five in number,
but have as their band of brothers,
every righteous man on earth.
That war is for later…

For now, remember,
the battle will be on two fronts,
and one will be your destiny.

BRIHANALLA:

Not mine, I cannot fight.

KRISHNA:

Fight you must.
Your brothers pack anger and raw strength.
But Karna and the rest have not been idle.
They possess terrible weapons
and won't hesitate to employ
that which will strengthen Duryodhana's resolve.
Only you possess the missiles of destruction
which can absolve this encounter.
Defeat the Kuru army
and create a minor victory.
For this, as I warned, is the dress rehearsal.
We have a need to weaken Duryodhana's obduracy,
and make Karna question his tenacity.
That will be the goal of this fight.
And without you, it cannot be done.
So, remember,
all your brothers, if they choose, can rest their arms.
But when the battle begins, you must be there.
When the line is drawn,
you must sound the alarm
that the Pandavas are alive
and, by God, have arrived.

BRIHANALLA:

Should Virata then be warned?
The death of Kichaka has weakened him substantially,
and the army is quite demoralised.
Maybe Bhima can start mustering the troops.
He is good at it.

KRISHNA:

No, don't play into Duryodhana's hands.
Remember, he still can quote obsolete calculations
and decadent practices,
and claim the exile is unfinished.
So, no, don't breathe a word.
Let the attack be launched.
And then respond as one must
in times of peril.
Not more. Not less.

BRIHANALLA:

Krishna, our weapons need to be fetched.

KRISHNA:

Do not worry.
A strange glow emits from where the weapons lie,
where you placed them on top of that hideous tree.
People fear going near.
Afraid of ghouls and ghosts.
The weapons know Arjuna.
They will be in call soon,
and have begun to radiate their preparation.
You will have ample time to fetch what is yours.

Brihanalla:

So, it's time, Krishna.

Krishna:

It always is… time.

Scene 7

DRAUPADI:

Bhoominjay… Prince Bhoominjay…
It's an attack from the north.
The Kurus have gathered our cattle,
and laid waste to the border villages.
The cowherds are fleeing in fear from the raging fire.
You need to assemble the men and counter the slaughter,
or before your father returns, it will all be over.

BHOOMINJAY:

If what you say is true, Sairandhari, then it's over,
for there are no men left.
All have gone to the southern frontier.
I have been assigned to protect the capital,
and I cannot leave my post. We know the Kurus
don't have too much respect for womenfolk.

All of you here are under my protection,
and to abandon this duty would be a disaster.
Send a messenger to the border.
Ask my father to spare us some soldiers.
This is an emergency.
It will be worth a battalion or two
to tackle the Kurus,
while I maintain my stoic place,
as guardian of the women and children.

DRAUPADI:

Impossible, Bhoominjay,
there is no time, or runners to spare.
You are the hope we must declare
to the battle forces, arrayed in expectation.
This is no time for dialectics and semantics.
Arise and stop this turbulent malevolence,
lest your father return to a smouldering graveyard.

BHOOMINJAY:

Sairandhari, do you believe I am making excuses?
We haven't even a charioteer to spare.
Women… what do you know or care?
This is not a doll's game where we can arrange and align
the stories to suit our aesthetics and expressions.
This is war.
It's Bhishma and Drona and Duryodhana you talk of.
Other things being equal,
I can match them arrow for arrow.
But the odds are now in their favour,
and my chance is too narrow

to win on foot.
Give me a charioteer,
and I am your man.
What Kurus? Even the gods with their weapons
will have to bow before the curve of my bow.
Go, and don't spread panic.
We will be stoic
and pray for the safe return of my father and his men.
Then, we will take on the Kurus,
and make them an early exit choose.

DRAUPADI:

My darling prince, why did you not say this before?
We have a brilliant charioteer,
right here in our midst.
And if a charioteer is all you need,
then gear up while I get your chariot fixed.

BHOOMINJAY:

We have someone in our midst?
Who is this hidden wonder?
Bring him to me.

DRAUPADI:

Brihanalla, it is.

BHOOMINJAY:

How dare you recommend a dancer,
to accompany me to war?
You want my enemies to laugh at me,
and dismiss me as a travesty?
I cannot indulge your pitiful recommendation.

What a whim!
To be driven in war
by a dancing… person.

Draupadi:

You are mistaken.
Brihanalla took to dance as a profession
because of his oath
to never drive the chariot again,
after his master lost his fortune to evil times.
Brihanalla is a master charioteer,
taught by the king of Madra himself.
He is as good as Krishna and Nakula,
when it comes to steeds.
You should ask him to navigate your way.
And trust me on this, Prince:
When Brihanalla drives, you will never go astray.

Bhoominjay:

Whose chariot has he driven,
that you give him so much respect?
What honours has he won with his skills,
that I should consider him my guide?

Draupadi:

He was Arjuna's charioteer.
He was Arjuna's navigator
when the Khandava burned for thirteen days and nights.
He was Arjuna's mate
when Arjuna went on his world campaign.
You cannot do better.

Call him, request him to support you.
And on a chariot driven by him,
you will fare as well as Arjuna would.
Why, some say Brihanalla was Arjuna's strength in battle,
while others say
not much separates the one from the other.

BHOOMINJAY:

Stop. I am sold.
Inform Brihanalla to wear the armour,
and approach me here.
We will draw the plan,
and make for the plains.
Fine, Sairandhari, you can have your way.

(*Draupadi exits.*)

Today is the day
I will protect all that is pure.
Bamboo arrows, please, with eagle fletching,
load sixteen quivers upon my chariot,
a few strong bows, and iron lances,
and my uncle Kichaka's mace.
Spineless enemies
who believe their path will be unobstructed
need to know this now.
They will be challenged, routed and demolished.
The glory will be mine today.
Ask Brihanalla to come here, quickly,
before the cattle is driven too far.

We need to accost them, stop them,
and give them, by God, a lovely war.

(*Draupadi enters, leading Brihanalla.*)

BRIHANALLA:

Prince, I am sorry. I have no idea what this maid told you,
but I cannot drive for anyone but my chosen master.

BHOOMINJAY:

Brihanalla, it is an order.
The salt you have eaten commands you.
Prepare the chariot, and let me ascend.
Drive me to the Kurus, and I promise you,
we will defend all that is ours.
Do not worry, I won't let you feel
the lack of a worthy master.
Arjuna is renowned,
but some of us, like diamonds,
stay hidden to be revealed,
only when the conditions are extreme.
Wear the armour, and let us proceed.

BRIHANALLA:

I have never worn an armour as Arjuna's charioteer,
for he never allowed any arrow to reach
within ten yards of me.
And, I am afraid, cannot wear one even if needed.
But, if you insist,
then I will need some help.

BHOOMINJAY:

Sure… I will tie it for you
as if you were the warrior and I, your valet.

DRAUPADI:

Brihanalla, Princess Uttara has sent word.
She needs the upper garments of all the Kuru kings
to decorate her latest dolls.
So, she asks for all the silks
to be gathered
once her brother has won the war.

BRIHANALLA:

Prince, why don't you promise your sister
the silken gifts,
and meet me by the city gates?
Let me harness the horses and arrange your weapons,
and we will leave for this auspicious cause.

(*Bhoominjay exits.*)

DRAUPADI:

The game is set, and you know how it will proceed.
Remember, this is not the day of judgement.
Do not exhaust all your anger.
Proceed without fanfare,
and let there be no drums or celebrations.
Remember, Duryodhana must face indignity, not death.
There are vows your brothers took,
and they must be redeemed by them another day.
And… return safe.

Scene Eight

BRIHANALLA:

Bhishma leads the phalanx, so we will try to avoid
the direct line of confrontation.
It would be prudent to attempt
to rip the left formation first,
and once we are in their midst,
you will have the advantage of surprise.
Would you like to call out a challenge?
Take them one by one.
Your horses are good,
and can take the strain.

BHOOMINJAY:

May I suggest we turn back; this battle is not for me.
I am fainting at the sight of those fluttering flags.
These warriors are renowned and too many.

I am shivering in my bones…
and not from the cold.
Why has the whole pantheon assembled?
And in such tremendous might?
Drona, Bhishma, Kripa, Karna,
Ashwatthama and Duryodhana.
Uttering their names
makes my tongue go dry.
And my fingers are not cooperating.
My bow slips from my hands,
and life seems too sweet to be squandered on the
battlefield.
Brihanalla, turn the horses.
I assure you these are
quite graceful in retreat too.
They will mistake us for reconnaissance spies,
and await the bigger attack.
There will be no shame attached.
Let us forfeit.

Brihanalla:

Do not be so scared.
Why are you raising your enemy's hopes,
even before the conch is blown?
We are yet to enter the arena of the fight.
It was your eager banter which prompted this encounter.
And you did pass that order with a flourish.
You forced me to obey you,
and I have done so.
Their banners and flags exhibit

more courage than you, Warrior Prince.
These hostile hordes show arrogance,
in raising their flags in your territory.
You cannot allow that to pass.
Prince, breathe and compose yourself.
This is war.
It's normal to be scared.
But act for the higher cause, the greater good.
We are but mere dolls
moved by higher powers.
We must act upon the moment…
not resist and deny.
We cannot return without the cattle.
And look, it's still in the enemy's hands.
To go back without a fight,
when you and I have been praised to the skies,
is unworthy. So, gather your courage and your bow,
and let me take you into the eye of the needle,
where Duryodhana nestles, protected by his army.
Shoot as I point and direct.
And if you die, die with glory.

Bhoominjay:

Are you crazy? There is no need for a fight.
Let the Kurus have the cows.
We must leave now, before they spot us.

Brihanalla:

A prince, a warrior,
speaking of fleeing?
Death would be more befitting.

Flight from fear?
Prince, arise, awake, and seize the day.
Let us fight.

BHOOMINJAY:

Fine.
One hundred coins of gold,
to return without a word.
We can pass the day in some nearby village,
and return to say,
we lost our way,
and did not find the place of battle.

BRIHANALLA:

Prince, if you fear fighting,
listen to me.
The wealth of your nation is at peril
and your enemies are not going to go without battle.
They will march into our lands,
and then there will be destruction.
I have a plan.
You drive the chariot.
I will fight. I will guard you,
while you make way,
through that inscrutable phalanx.
Those warriors are of mettle,
but not undefeatable.
I will fight and recover the bovine.
Will you agree to drive the chariot?
Or, would you prefer to rest behind that tree
while I proceed on foot to fight?

BHOOMINJAY:

I will drive the chariot.
You can use my weapons.
I give you permission.

BRIHANALLA:

These are not suitable for me.
The bows are too flimsy.
Let me tell you a secret.
You see this tree?
Amidst its foliage is hidden a bundle
that resembles a corpse,
and it emits a blue light.
Chant this incantation,
and allow the bundle to show itself.
Bring it to me.

BHOOMINJAY:

You want me to carry a dead body?

BRIHANALLA:

All of us do,
through our lives,
never realising the mirth of the truth.
Do not worry, it's not a corpse,
but weapons for war.

BHOOMINJAY:

This is not a magic spectacle, right?
These are weapons of the sort I have only heard about.
Who owns them?
And are we using them with permission?

Who can use these weapons?
They seem heavy and inspire awe in me.
Is there a mystery here I am unable to perceive?
Tell me, how do you know all this,
and the spell to receive
these magnificent weapons?

BRIHANALLA:

It is a secret,
and I am trusting you,
when I reveal to you,
that the owners of these weapons
are five brothers
who will return to claim them.
For now, we are borrowing them.

BHOOMINJAY:

Are you suggesting what I am thinking?
That these belong to the scions of the house of the Kurus?
That these are the jewels of the sons of Pandu?

BRIHANALLA:

You are a smart boy.
Yes, that's correct.
And today, we will be collecting the weapons of Arjuna,
to fight those wonderful men,
who are getting edgy and fidgeting,
and will commence the attack any moment.

BHOOMINJAY:

If the weapons are here,
they must be close too.

Brihanalla:

Maybe...

Bhoominjay:

I am Bhoominjay Uttara Kumar,
son of the Matsya king
and I will be driving that chariot in this battle.
Whom do I have the honour of serving?
Who is my warrior?
With what name will I announce you to the enemies?
What banner would you like me to unfurl?
Allow me this information,
which I demand as a battle charioteer.

Brihanalla:

Announce your warrior
with the Rishabha note on the conch.
Unfurl the standard of the ape.
Do not worry about wearing an armour,
for no arrow will come within ten yards of you.
Announce me as the warrior with no name.
Shall we proceed now?

Bhoominjay:

Arjuna... I am confused...
is it really you,
whom I thought to be a dancing teacher all this time?

Brihanalla:

I am Arjuna.

BHOOMINJAY:

Indulge this foolish boy
and repeat the ten names of Arjuna and their origins.
It will fill me with courage and joy.

BRIHANALLA:

And test whether I am the real person? Well done!
I am:
Arjuna, for I was born under the Arjuna tree.
Partha, for my mother is Pritha.
Phalguna, the month I was born in.
Jishnu, as I am invincible.
Kiritin, as I wear the crown Indra placed upon me.
Shwetavahana, for my chariot and steeds are white.
Dhananjaya, for I have collected wealth.
Savyasachin, for I am ambidextrous.
Vibhatsu, for I have never committed an act of repugnance.
And Krishna, for my dark skin.

BHOOMINJAY:

It is my fortune that I have met you.
My ignorance, you must forgive.
Strangely, I am not afraid anymore.
Command me!
Where would you like me to direct the horses?
Your appearance and guise are yet to offer me answers.
But great persons have great cause,
to do what they do.
I seek no more answers.
I will yoke the horses
and let us to battle.

Scene Nine

DRAUPADI:

How many wounds
are you capable of carrying on your body?
A few arrows have pierced you, and exited too.

BRIHANALLA:

They are not invincible, Draupadi.
I fought them all at once.
I defeated them in quick succession.
I was helped because they were fighting among themselves.
Ashwatthama seemed more intent
on Karna's throat than mine.
The cattle were rustled
even as Duryodhana tried to hustle away in stealth.
And all the men now are sleeping blissfully in the dust.
Once the chemicals' effect wears away,

they will go back as quickly as they came.
Our purpose has been achieved manifold.
Matsya is safe and Virata is indebted.
Bhoominjay is a diehard devotee.
And Karna knows that
he cannot defeat me.

DRAUPADI:

What about Drona and the brahmana hordes?

BRIHANALLA:

They stay for Bhishma and the king's grace
upon their plates and homes.
Their heart was not in the fight.

DRAUPADI:

Your brother has sent a message.
He wants us to appear in court tomorrow
without our disguise.
The period is safely done with, months ago in fact.
Now, we are all free
to appear as who we are.
So, tomorrow morning we congregate,
address the court of Matsya,
and thank them for their hospitality.
So, tonight, say goodbye to your disciples.

BRIHANALLA:

My life has been a series of exiles.
I was born when my father
was in self-imposed banishment.
Then, for fear of the Kurus, we stayed away.

Later, we met you while begging for food.
I was sent away for transgressing the bedroom rules.
We lost at dice, and it was to the forest again.
And then my singular quest for weapons of destruction.
And now, finally, this year in disguise.
Now, we can look forward to never again
being away from home.

DRAUPADI:

It is still a long way off, Arjuna.
That irreplaceable joy
won't be attained without endeavour.
We will have to walk through blood and gore.
And you will have to conduct the sacrifice
where your arrows will be the incantations.
The blood, the oblations,
and the battlefield, the holy fire
to give us absolution.
Tomorrow is the beginning of the day we lived for.
Tomorrow, I will breathe in joy.

BRIHANALLA:

We have a prisoner, Draupadi.

DRAUPADI:

You got a Kuru with you?

BRIHANALLA:

A Kuru, a Pandu and a Yadu.

DRAUPADI:

Abhimanyu?

BRIHANALLA:

I captured him in a good duel.
He is not bad at all.
Almost as sharp as Satyaki
and Pradyumna.
I am proud of his strength.

DRAUPADI:

The father was missing his son.

BRIHANALLA:

The son was sought by the father-in-law.

DRAUPADI:

Whose father-in-law?

BRIHANALLA:

Uttara.

(*Uttara enters.*)

UTTARA:

Sairandhari, go quickly to the court.
The king and Kanka are having an argument.
I fear my father will lose his temper,
and insult that good man, Kanka.
Please go now.

BRIHANALLA:

Sairandhari, do as the princess demands,
and make sure that Kanka stays in control.

Ensure that the king's anger is defused,
and make those venerable men see peace.
Princess Uttara, what are they fighting about?

UTTARA:

The king wanted to weigh Bhoominjay in gold,
and distribute the coins to the land's needy.
So pleased he is with my brother's victory.
But Kanka kept reiterating that Brihanalla is the presence
which can keep defeat away.
Victory is always assured, when Brihanalla leads the way.

BRIHANALLA:

Kanka made the king angry
by speaking words of distaste.

UTTARA:

Not words of lies.

BRIHANALLA:

Princess, your brother fought well today.
And won the battle and the day.

UTTARA:

And still, my brother has no wounds on his body,
and you are covered with arrow shots.
The plumage on them tells me the tales
of all the warriors who must have targeted you today.

BRIHANALLA:

No, Princess, sometimes, some warriors, a little nervous,
shoot at the charioteer in fear.

Uttara:

Not Karna, not Drona…
and no, Brihanalla,
definitely, not Bhishma.

(She holds up Bhishma's arrow)

Brihanalla:

Before this conversation becomes difficult, let's desist.
Princess Uttara, please return to your room.
I will dress my wounds and proceed to meet the king.

Uttara:

I will await you tomorrow.
We will have our class as usual.

Brihanalla:

I believe the king has called a special assembly.
I will come to meet you once that is over.
And, did your brother give you the famous silks?

Uttara:

The brother has gifted me with the cloth.
But where is my master's present?
You did not bring me anything
from such a tremendous battle.

Brihanalla:

But I did.
And tomorrow, I will give you not one
but two gifts.

Uttara:

I will accept any gift you give me.
Inopportune or not,
I will await your word,
your presence,
your moment with me, Brihanalla.
Tomorrow will throw a few surprises.
So, tonight, forgive me.
For anything I may have said
as your master's daughter,
may have been said in folly.
What seemed like a misfortune
now perches on the threshold of historical truth.
Let it be a gift, my teacher,
that I receive from you,
for no one but you knows my inner desire,
exposed to you in a moment of truth.
Tonight will be difficult to pass.
But I will meditate and pray.
So, when we all awake tomorrow,
it will be the start of a glorious day.

Scene Ten

Uttara:

You? Please go away.
I am now to be your daughter-in-law,
wife of Abhimanyu.
The Kurus sought the cattle,
and you sought the woman.
I presume all of you have had your resolution.
My father offered you my hand in marriage.
You could have said no, and moved away.
Why did you have to ask me for Abhimanyu?
He is your son.
How can I be the consort of a man
whose father I desired?
What is this heinous thing you have done?
No longer are you Vibhatsu,

for this is a repugnant act.
So what if it was not on a battlefield?
Life in these times is no less than a war.
Now, I will have to see your face everyday,
after having been with your son,
and shared his bed.
Did you tell your son?
"To the woman who desired me,
I am offering the next best thing,
you, who are a living image of me.
Marry her, and seal this treaty,
and we will have a whole regiment
of Matsya's best,
when we take the battlefield with your uncles."
I am condemned to a life of desperation,
to be with a man I never wanted,
and all because you were too cowardly to marry me.

ARJUNA:

And what would have been the answer,
to the tongues that would have spun stories
of what possibly occurred in the guise
of dance and drama tutelage?
That Arjuna was having an affair
with a girl a quarter his age?
The king of Matsya believed he was doing the right thing
in offering you in marriage.
But he forgot we have been intimate
for a whole year.
That would be a blot on the teacher-student communion.

People would sneer
that Arjuna converted the teaching space
into his personal harem.
Uttara, this was the best step to take
to avoid offending the pride of the Matsyas
or making them feel violated.
Now, the marriage will settle doubts of sanctity,
and profanity will not find a place.
The teacher and the student will not be disgraced.
You are my student
and will always be my loving child.
And I did not lie
when I said I loved you.

UTTARA:

Please go away from here.
I would ask you to get out, but I am afraid
the valuable Kuru blood would be offended.
And we will have to dread its vengeance.
No, Prince Arjuna, thank you
for your ruthless consideration.
I am but an aberration,
in your perfect life.
For one who refused Urvashi,
what can a poor girl like me inspire?
What can I offer you in the bower of love,
that you have not tasted or appreciated?
Please go away, father-in-law.
The rules you are so fond of
do not allow us to talk and negotiate.

ARJUNA:

Uttara… or Princess Uttara if you will.
My life is not mine to steer.
I don't have the luxury of making decisions
without the permission of history and my elders.
It's not within the happiness and fortune
of everyone
to be a human.
Some are condemned to be gods,
and must bear the condemnation
in life and beyond.

UTTARA:

Then, God, tell me this:
What must I do,
when I love you,
not your son?
And now, I will be a receptacle,
and bear your grandchildren.
Please do me one favour, one request your student has,
and if you do love me the way you say you do,
then please stay away
and let me never see your face.
For every time I see you, I weaken.
My resolve will crumble,
and I will not be dutiful
to Abhimanyu.
Promise me this:
After today,
never again to come

face to face.
Understand this, Great God,
Uttara fell in love
once in her life,
and that was with you.
Now, she will endeavour to hide that affection
and put on a guise to serve your son.
And it will not be easy at all.
Like you were in a vitality-lacking guise for a year,
I will be mirthless for life.
Poor Abhimanyu,
make sure he has more wives.
For Uttara can never be to him
what she thought she would be to you.
Thank you.
Now please go away, father-in-law.

ARJUNA:

Fortunate are those who are born simple,
and live life as they wish.
For those of us condemned to be history's slaves,
we will live and die by its pages.
I bless you, daughter-in-law.
May you be happy in life.

UTTARA:

Last evening, I knew who you were.
I did not sleep the entire night.
For I was dreaming and crafting plays
where you would be recognised by the king,
and then would ask for my hand in marriage,

and I would be your queen.
I was dreaming of the yellow thread
that Draupadi would tie around my wrist,
and how Bhima would tease me,
the Twins lift me in jest,
and Yudhishthira bless me.
But my dreams had the last laugh.
I am to get everything,
and nothing.

ARJUNA:

Uttara don't think badly of me.
I never saw you as a lover.
While I did love you,
wanted your happiness,
and in all tenderness,
I saw you in my home
with my son as your lover.
I will march tomorrow to the war camp,
and then it will be the soldier's strife.
Only when we cousins resolve our conflict
will I return to domestic life.
Or maybe I won't.
Maybe I will die in battle,
and reach for the glories of the sky.
But I promise you,
as long as I am on the field of battle,
Abhimanyu will not be harmed.
You will lead a beautiful life,
and all the happiness in this world will be yours.

Uttara:

Lies.
Blatant lies.
Leave now, please,
before I slit my wrist in disgust
for the sorry figure you cut before me.
I would rather you slapped me
and asked me to behave
than promise me unwarranted things.
Be who you are, Arjuna.
Afford me that respect at least.
You served your purpose in the dancing hall.
You broke my heart.
Now don't attack my spirit.
Let that at least stay true and unmutilated.
And do tell Mother Draupadi,
I too know what it is
to be violated.

Scene Eleven

DRAUPADI:

Krishna, is there any woman on earth like me?
I was born by the grace of the gods,
born daughter of a warrior king,
twin sister of another.
I am the mother of five sons
whom you hold as beloved
as Abhimanyu, your sister's son.
And yet, I was dragged by my hair,
and insulted before my husbands' gaze.
Treated like a slave,
while my five husbands sat mute,
without feeling a speck of angst or anger.
Only when I took your name
was Dhritarashtra awakened to the crime.

He was silently enjoying the spectacle.
Morally, I am the daughter-in-law of the house of the Kurus
and yet, was made a slave.
Would the Pandavas watch Uttara undergo such shame?
Then why was I so unfortunate?
If the Kauravas are going to live
on the same earth as I, then shame.
Shame, shame, shame, shame,
on my husbands and their gallantry and battle skills.
What makes them ask you to sue for peace?
Krishna, if you have ever loved me, and believe
I deserve some favour from you,
then don't carry this message of peace to the Kurus.
Tell them it's war
and then, kill them.
Tell my husbands not to be anxious for peace.
For all seems happy and clean,
when the belly is full,
the lips red with betel,
and the wedding feast being digested.
But we owe a debt to this earth.
See my hair that has become a snake,
when it was held by Dushasana in his rude hands.
My husbands have sunk so low
as to obliterate it from their living memory.
Fine, then, my aged father and my sons,
along with my brother will fight.
My son, Abhimanyu, born of Subhadra, will fight.
I have no peace.
Where can I gather peace?

Not in the diplomacy
in which my husbands seek refuge.
Let me be crass, let me be crude.
I seek Duryodhana's death, and Dushasana's blood.
Thirteen years this smouldering fire has thrived,
expecting better times to come.
I have hidden my wrath,
knowing my husbands will give it vent.
And now, they ask you to go,
and talk of peace,
in return for five villages.
My heart will break, Krishna.

KRISHNA:

Why this desolation, Draupadi?
Why are you giving way to base emotions?
Come, sit next to me, and listen.
Tell me, what do you hear?

DRAUPADI:

The wedding songs of Uttara and Abhimanyu
as they move from person to person,
seeking blessings and benedictions.
The joyous dance of the ecstatic uncles,
the sounds of the mridangas and the flute,
sounds of fulfilment and contentment.
I hear lassitude.
I hear the satisfaction of men,
who will be satisfied with less.
I hear them shutting the doors,
on their past, their vows and oaths,

which sounded robust enough
when made with boiling blood.
But now, they are well-fed and pampered,
and have forgotten
all they promised to achieve and do.

KRISHNA:

Listen deeper, Draupadi.
Extend your ears further.
Close your eyes and listen.
You will hear conch shells and battle drums.
You will hear agonising shrieks and the sound of death.
The war is close.
It is a strong wind that blows.
And edifices will fall, men will fall.
And will fall the gathered knowledge of our past.
But fall they must,
for truth to stay
and stabilize the earth.

DRAUPADI:

If you say so.
I don't believe anything anymore.
I am disappointed and devastated
by my husbands and their call for peace.
They have forgotten,
in their joy of welcoming Uttara,
the new daughter-in-law,
that their clan does not have a good record
as daughters-in-law go.

Krishna:

They asked for five villages.

Draupadi:

How benevolent!
The ruler of the earth
now wants five villages.
What for? To play dice in peace?
One skirmish and Arjuna is satisfied!
How manly to build-up dark clouds, and threaten havoc,
and then rain down in an instant
and feel liberated!
How manly to scream and shout of killing all,
and then with one encounter
believe it is requited!
Krishna, you killed Shishupala,
to ensure they remained unchallenged.
You went out to accept their sovereignty,
for your love of your cousins.
And now, it's all wasted.
They want five villages to retire and rest?
I don't want five villages.
I don't want a kingdom or gold or cows.
I want the blood of the Kaurava brothers.
And after that is delivered,
I will leave on my own to the forest.
Yudhishthira is modest and anxious for peace.
I am not.
I crave severe retaliation
against all those

who made us slaves.
Krishna, give me what was promised
to me thirteen years ago.
It was not a kingdom, nor five villages.
It was revenge.

KRISHNA:

"Kushasthala, Vrikasthala,
Makandi, Varnavata,
and the fifth,
any you desire."
That is what the elder Pandu said.
He has not forgotten anything, Draupadi.
He asks for the village where Bhima was poisoned.
He asks for the village where an assassination attempt on them was made.
He asks for the village where the game of dice was played.
He asks for the place where you ruled.
And he says a fifth by your choice,
to make up for all the other crimes perpetuated.
They who have angered you
are already dead, Draupadi.
Do not judge your husbands
for what they speak in diplomacy.
That is the etiquette of kings.
To offer every possible chance to their enemies
before they annihilate them.
It has been ordained, the deaths of all those men,
and it will be accomplished by me.
The hour has made its call.

And if the sons of Dhritarashtra do not listen to my words,
then they will lie on the battlefield
as food for jackals and dogs.
Do not cry, Draupadi, my words are not futile.
I swear to you, your enemies will be killed.

The Past

Scene Twelve

(*Draupadi stands with her hands held above her head.*)

DRAUPADI:

Govinda, Govinda, Govinda…

THE END

Acknowledgements

My salutations to the writers, story-tellers and playwrights whose works have inspired me all my life to explore the squillion aspects of *The Mahabharata* again and again. I would like to express my gratitude to the prodigious translations of the epic by Kisari Mohan Ganguli, M N Dutt and Bibek Debroy. I would also like to acknowledge being inspired by Anupam Kumar's *Brihanalla,* which I had the opportunity to act in, in the year 1996.

Photo: M Sivanesan

V Balakrishnan is an actor, playwright, designer and an ICCR empaneled director. An alumnus of the Shri Ram Centre for Performing Arts and the National School of Drama, New Delhi, he is a Charles Wallace Scholar and a recipient of the Fulbright Distinguished Award in Teaching. Balakrishnan is the founder and artistic director of Theatre Nisha, Chennai, and has over 200 productions to his credit. His play *Sordid* won The Hindu Playwright Award 2019.

www.ingramcontent.com/pod-product-compliance
Ingram Content Group UK Ltd.
Pitfield, Milton Keynes, MK11 3LW, UK
UKHW041843200726
13854UKWH00005BA/2047

9 788195 439911